A Treasury of Wisdom copyright © Frances Lincoln Limited 2002

First published in Great Britain in 2002 by
Frances Lincoln Limited, 4 Torriano Mews
Torriano Avenue, London NW5 2RZ

and in the United States by Ignatius Press, San Francisco

For photographic acknowledgements and copyright details, see page 77

Library of Congress control number 2001094401

ISBN 0-89870-912-1

Words and images chosen by Yvonne Whiteman
Designed by Becky Clarke
Set in Perpetua

Printed in Singapore
1 3 5 7 9 8 6 4 2

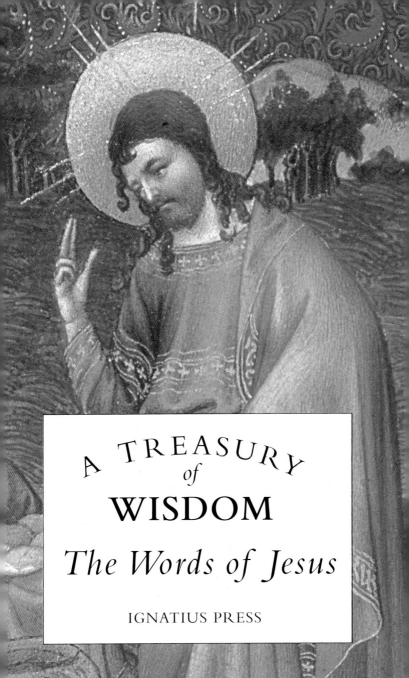

A TREASURY *of* WISDOM

The Words of Jesus

IGNATIUS PRESS

"**B**ut take heed,
I have told you all things beforehand."

St Mark 13:23

CONTENTS

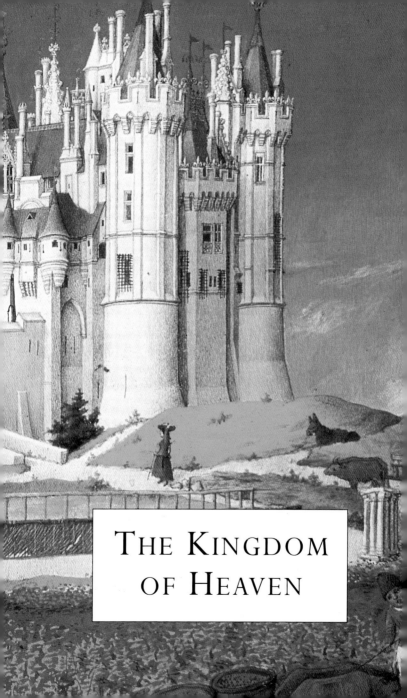

THE KINGDOM
OF HEAVEN

"Truly, I say to you, whoever does not receive the kingdom of God like a child shall not enter it."

St Luke 18: 17

"Again I tell you, it is easier for a camel to go through the eye of a needle than for a rich man to enter the kingdom of God."
When the disciples heard this they were greatly astonished, saying, "Who then can be saved?"
But Jesus looked at them and said to them,
"With men this is impossible,
but with God all things are possible."

St Matthew 19: 24-26

" For the kingdom of heaven is like a householder who went out early in the morning to hire laborers for his vineyard. After agreeing with the laborers for a denarius a day, he sent them into his vineyard.

And going out about the third hour he saw others standing idle in the market place; and to them he said 'You go into the vineyard too, and whatever is right I will give you.' So they went.

Going out again about the sixth hour and the ninth hour he did the same.

And about the eleventh hour he went out and found others standing; and he said to them,
'Why do you stand here idle all day?'
They said to him, 'Because no one has hired us.'
He said to them, 'You go into the vineyard too.'

And when evening came, the owner of the vineyard said to his steward, 'Call the laborers and pay them their wages, beginning with the last, up to the first.'

And when those hired about the eleventh hour came, each of them received a denarius.

Now when the first came, they thought they would receive more; but each of them also received a denarius. And on receiving it they grumbled at the householder, saying, 'These last worked only one hour, and you have made them equal to us who have borne the burden of the day and the scorching heat.' But he replied to one of them,

'Friend, I am doing you no wrong; did you not agree with me for a denarius? Take what belongs to you and go; I choose to give to this last as I give to you. Am I not allowed to do what I choose with what belongs to me? Or do you begrudge my generosity?' So the last will be first, and the first last."

St Matthew 20: 1-16

"Let the children come to me, do not hinder them; for to such belongs the kingdom of God."

St Mark 10: 14

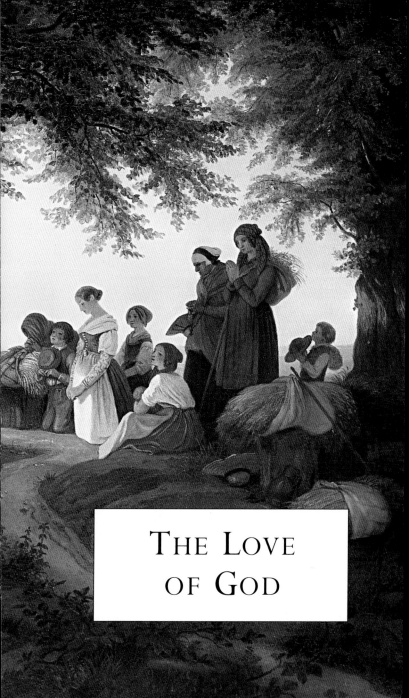

THE LOVE
OF GOD

"Pray then like this:

O ur Father who art in heaven,
Hallowed be thy name.
Thy kingdom come.
Thy will be done,
  On earth as it is in heaven.
Give us this day our daily bread;
And forgive us our trespasses,
  As we forgive those who trespass against us;
And lead us not into temptation,
  But deliver us from evil."

St Matthew 6: 9-13

"Ask, and it will be given you; seek, and you will find; knock, and it will be opened to you.

For every one who asks receives, and he who seeks finds, and to him who knocks it will be opened."

St Luke 11: 9-10

"And why are you anxious about clothing? Consider the lilies of the field, how they grow; they neither toil nor spin; yet I tell you, even Solomon in all his glory was not clothed like one of these.

But if God so clothes the grass of the field, which today is alive and tomorrow is thrown into the oven, will he not much more clothe you, O men of little faith?"

St Matthew 6: 28-30

"What woman, having ten silver coins,
if she loses one coin, does not light
a lamp and sweep the house and seek
diligently until she finds it?
And when she has found it, she calls together
her friends and neighbors, saying,
'Rejoice with me, for I have found the coin
which I had lost.'
Just so, I tell you there is joy before the angels
of God over one sinner who repents."

St Luke 15: 8-10

And he said to his disciples,
"Therefore I tell you, do not be anxious
about your life, what you shall eat,
nor about your body, what you shall put on.
For life is more than food, and the body more
than clothing.
Consider the ravens: they neither sow nor reap,
they have neither storehouse nor barn,
and yet God feeds them.
Of how much more value are you than the birds!
And which of you by being anxious can add a cubit
to his span of life?
If then you are not able to do as small a thing
as that, why are you anxious about the rest?"

St Luke 12: 22-26

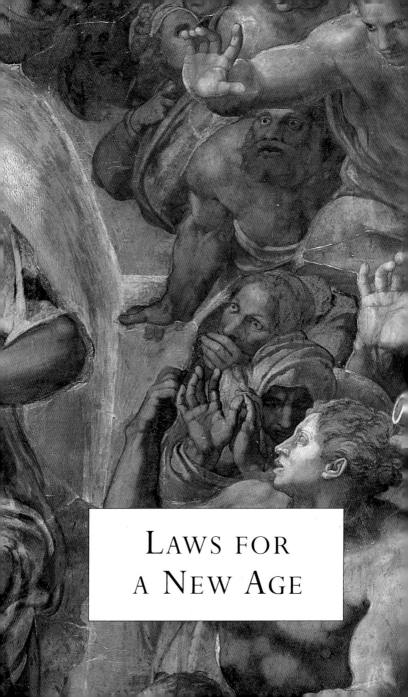

LAWS FOR
A NEW AGE

" 'You shall love the Lord your God
with all your heart, and with all
your soul, and with all your mind,
and with all your strength.'
The second is this,
'You shall love your neighbor as
yourself.' There is no other
commandment greater than these."

St Mark 12: 30-31

" This I command you,
to love one another."

St John 15: 17

"You have heard that it was said
to the men of old,
'You shall not kill; and whoever kills shall
be liable to judgment.'
But I say to you that every one who is angry
with his brother shall be liable to judgment."

St Matthew 5: 21-22

"Judge not, that you be not judged.
For with the judgment you
pronounce you will be judged,
and the measure you give
will be the measure you get."

St Matthew 7: 1-2

"Do not lay up for yourselves
treasures on earth, where
moth and rust consume and where
thieves break in and steal, but lay up
for yourselves treasures in heaven,
where neither moth nor rust
consumes and where thieves
do not break in and steal.
For where your treasure is,
there will your heart be also."

St Matthew 6: 19-21

"No one can serve two masters; for either he will hate the one and love the other, or he will be devoted to the one and despise the other.
You cannot serve God and mammon."

St Matthew 6: 24

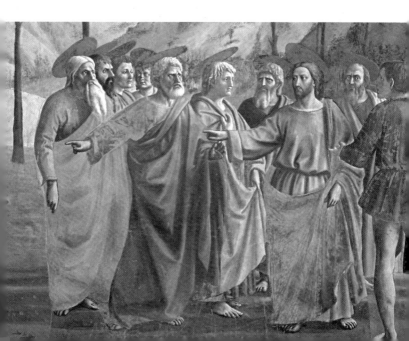

"Render … to Caesar the things that are Caesar's, and to God the things that are God's."

St Matthew 22: 21

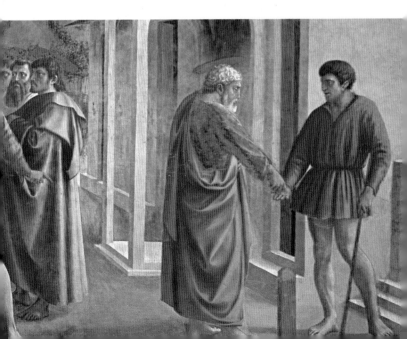

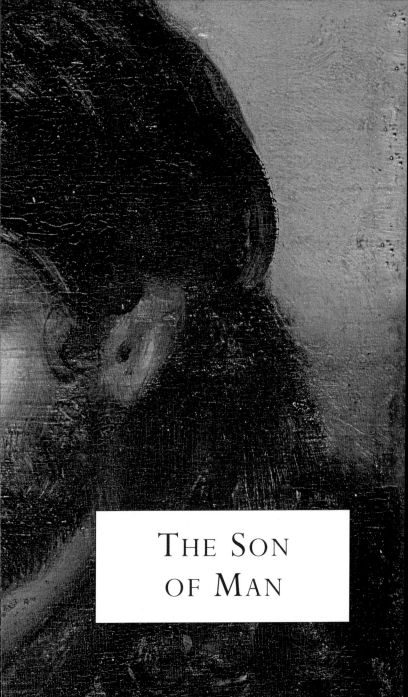

THE SON
OF MAN

And he told them many things in parables, saying;
"A sower went out to sow.
And as he sowed, some seeds fell along the path
and the birds came and devoured them.
Other seeds fell on rocky ground,
where they had not much soil and immediately
they sprang up, since they had no depth of soil,
but when the sun rose they were scorched;
and, since they had no root they withered away.
Other seeds fell upon thorns, and the thorns
grew up and choked them.
Other seeds fell on good soil
and brought forth grain, some a hundredfold,
some sixty, some thirty.
He who has ears, let him hear."

St Matthew 13: 3-9

"I am the light of the world; he who follows me will not walk in darkness, but will have the light of life."

St John 8: 12

"My kingship is not of this world;
if my kingship were of this world,
my servants would fight, that I might not
be handed over to the Jews; but my kingship
is not from the world."

St John 18: 36

"I am the good shepherd.
The good shepherd lays down
his life for the sheep."

St John 10: 11

"Those who are well have no need
for a physician, but those who are sick;
I have not come to call the righteous,
but sinners to repentance."

St Luke 5: 31-32

"Greater love has no man than this, that a man lay down his life for his friends."

St John 15: 13

"A man once gave a great banquet,
and invited many; and at the time for
the banquet he sent his servant to say
to those who had been invited,
'Come; for all is now ready.'
But they all alike began to make excuses....
Then the householder in anger said to his servant,
'Go out quickly to the streets and lanes
of the city, and bring in the poor and maimed
and blind and lame.'
And the servant said,
'Sir, what you commanded has been done,
and still there is room.'
And the master said to the servant,
'Go out to the highways and hedges,
and compel people to come in,
that my house may be filled.
For I tell you none of those men who were invited
shall taste my banquet.'"

St Luke 14: 16-24

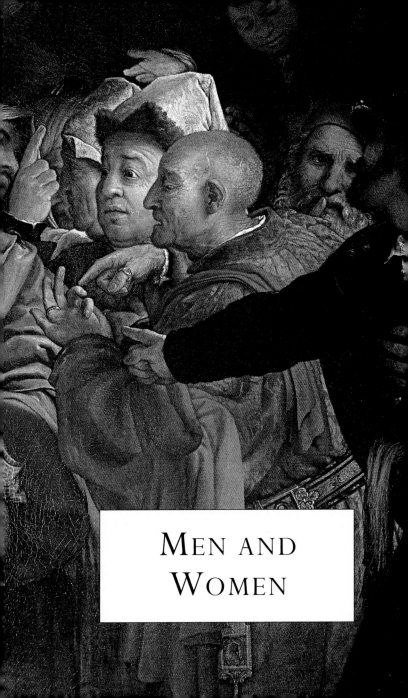

MEN AND WOMEN

"A man was going down from Jerusalem
to Jericho, and he fell among robbers,
who stripped him and beat him, and departed,
leaving him half dead.
Now by chance a priest was going down that road;
and when he saw him he passed by on
the other side.
So likewise a Levite, when he came to the place
and saw him, passed by on the other side.
But a Samaritan, as he journeyed, came to where
he was; and when he saw him, he had compassion,
and went to him and bound up his wounds,
pouring on oil and wine; then he set him on
his own beast and bought him to an inn,
and took care of him.
And the next day he took out two denarii
and gave them to the innkeeper, saying,
'Take care of him; and whatever more you spend,
I will repay you when I come back.'
Which of these three, do you think proved neighbor
to the man who fell among the robbers?"
…"Go and do likewise."

St Luke 10: 30-37

He said to Thomas, "Put your finger here, and see my hands; and put out your hand, and place it in my side; do not be faithless, but believing."

Thomas answered him, "My Lord and my God!"

Jesus said to him, "Have you believed because you have seen me?

Blessed are those who have not seen and yet believe."

St John 20: 27-29

Jesus said to him, "What do you want
me to do for you?"
And the blind man said to him, "Master, let
me receive my sight."
And Jesus said to him, "Go your way; your faith
has made you well."
And immediately he received his sight and
followed him on the way.

St Mark 10: 51-53

J esus said to him,
     "If you would be perfect, go, sell
     what you possess and give to the poor,
     and you will have treasure in heaven;
     and come, follow me."
When the young man heard this
     he went away sorrowful;
     for he had great possessions.

St Matthew 19: 21-22

H e stood up and said to them,
"Let him who is without sin
among you be the first to throw
a stone at her."
And once more he bent down and
wrote with his finger on the ground.
But when they heard it, they went
away, one by one, beginning with the
eldest, and Jesus was left alone with
the woman standing before him.
Jesus looked up and said to her,
"Woman, where are they? Has no
one condemned you?"
She said, "No one, Lord."
And Jesus said, "Neither do I condemn
you; go, and do not sin again."

St John 8: 7-11

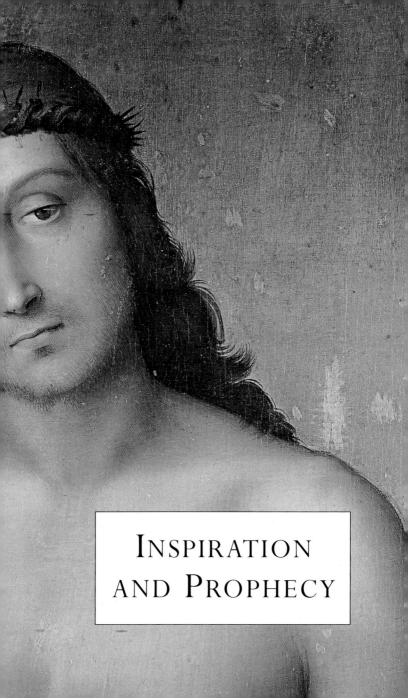

INSPIRATION
AND PROPHECY

"Blessed are the poor in spirit,
for theirs is the kingdom of heaven.
Blessed are those who mourn,
for they shall be comforted.
Blessed are the meek, for they shall inherit the earth.
Blessed are those who hunger and thirst
for righteousness, for they shall be satisfied.
Blessed are the merciful, for they shall obtain mercy.
Blessed are the pure in heart, for they shall see God.
Blessed are the peacemakers,
for they shall be called sons of God.
Blessed are those who are persecuted
for righteousness' sake,
for theirs is the kingdom of heaven.
Blessed are you when men revile you
and persecute you and utter all kinds of evil
against you falsely on my account.
Rejoice and be glad,
for your reward is great in heaven."

St Matthew 5: 3-12

"For what does it profit a man, to gain the whole world and forfeit his life?"

St Mark 8: 36

" Therefore I tell you,
    do not be anxious about your life,
  what you shall eat or what you shall drink,
    nor about your body, what you shall put on.
  Is not life more than food, and the body
    more than clothing?"

St Matthew 6: 25

" Every one who comes to me and hears my words and does them, I will show you what he is like: he is like a man building a house, who dug deep, and laid the foundation upon rock; and when a flood arose, the stream broke against that house, and could not shake it, because it had been well built.

But he who hears and does not do them is like a man who built a house on the ground without a foundation; against which the stream broke, and immediately it fell, and the ruin of that house was great."

St Luke 6: 47-49

"Beware of false prophets, who come to you in sheep's clothing but inwardly are ravenous wolves.

You will know them by their fruits.

Are grapes gathered from thorns,
    or figs from thistles?

    ...A sound tree cannot bear evil fruit,
    nor can a bad tree bear good fruit."

St Matthew 7: 15-16, 18

"I tell you, there will be more joy
in heaven over one sinner
who repents than over
ninety-nine righteous persons
who need no repentance."

St Luke 15: 7

"Heaven and earth will pass away: but my words will not pass away."

St Mark 13: 31

INDEX OF ARTISTS

AND PAINTINGS

ENDPAPERS
Primavera (detail)
Sandro Botticelli
(about 1445–1510)
Uffizi, Florence

PAGES 4 & 5
**The Multiplication of
Loaves and Fishes** (details)
(Ms. 65/1284, fol.168v)
Les Très Riches Heures du Duc
de Berry (early 15th century)
Musée Condé, Chantilly

PAGE 6
The Last Supper
School of Raphael
(1483–1520)
Vatican Loggias, Rome

PAGES 8-9
**September: Harvesting
Grapes** (detail)
(Ms.65/1284, fol.9v)
Les Très Riches Heures du Duc
de Berry (early 15th century)
Musée Condé, Chantilly

PAGE 10
Tobias and the Angel
(detail)
Francesco Botticini
(c.1446–1497)
Santa Maria del Fiore
Cathedral, Florence

PAGE 13
Procession of the Magi
(detail)
Benozzo Gozzoli (c.1421–1497)
Palazzo Medici-Riccardi,
Florence

PAGE 15
A Still Life with Grapes
(detail)
Gerardus van Spaendonck
(1746–1822)
Private Collection

PAGES 16-17
**Christ blessing
the Children** (detail)
Nicolaes Maes (1634–1693)
National Gallery, London

PAGES 18-19
**Prayer at a Chapel
in a Forest** (detail)
Ludwig Richter (1803–1884)
Location of painting unknown

PAGE 20
The Apostle Philip (detail)
Georges de la Tour
(1593–1652)
Chrysler Museum of Art,
Norfolk, Virginia

PAGE 22
Female Donor Portrait
(detail)
(from the **Cycle of St Francis**)
Domenico Ghirlandaio (1449–1494)
Sassetti Chapel, Santa Trinita,
Florence

PAGE 23
Bouquet de Lys en Pied
(detail)
Frank Bramley (1857–1915)
Private Collection

PAGES 24-25
**The Parable of the
Lost Coin** (detail)
Domenico Feti
(c.1589–1623)
Gemäldegalerie, Dresden

PAGE 27
A Concert of Birds (detail)
German School (18th century)
Private Collection

PAGES 28–29
Christ (detail from
The Last Judgement)
Michelangelo (1475–1564)
Sistine Chapel, Vatican, Rome

PAGE 30
**The Return of the
Prodigal Son** (detail)
Lionello Spada (1576–1622)
Louvre, Paris

PAGE 31
The Visitation
Mariotto Albertinelli
(1474–1515)
Uffizi, Florence

PAGES 32-33
**Portrait of Two
Young Men** (detail)
Attributed to Giovanni Cariani
(1480/85?–1547?)
Louvre, Paris

PAGES 34-35
**The Adoration of
the Kings** (detail)
Sandro Botticelli (1445–1510)
Uffizi, Florence

PAGES 36-37
The Tribute Money (detail)
Masaccio
(1401–probably1428)
Brancacci Chapel, Santa Maria
del Carmine, Florence

PAGES 38-39
Head of Christ (detail)
School of Rembrandt
(1606–1669)
Staatliche Museen zu Berlin
Preussischer Kulturbesitz,
Gemäldegalerie

PAGE 40
The Sower
Jean-François Millet
(1814–1875)
Museum of Fine Arts, Boston

PAGES 42-43
**Christ Walking on
the Waters** (detail)
Julius Sergius Klever
(1850–1924)
Private Collection

PAGE 44
Minding the Flock (detail)
Cornelis van Leemputten
(1841–1902)
Private Collection

PAGE 45
The Deposition (detail)
Michelangelo Merisi da
Caravaggio (1571–1610)
Pinacoteca, Vatican, Rome

PAGES 46-47
Head of Christ (detail)
Correggio
(about 1494; died 1534)
The J. Paul Getty Museum,
Los Angeles

PAGE 48
**A Large Company feasting
outside a House** (detail)
Gillis van Tilborch
(1625–1678)
Private Collection

PAGES 50-51
**Christ and the Woman
taken in Adultery** (detail)
Lorenzo Lotto (1480–1556)
Louvre, Paris

PAGE 52
The Good Samaritan
(detail)
Circle of Antonio Zanchi
(1631–1722)
Private Collection

PAGE 54
**The Doubting of Saint
Thomas** (detail from central
panel of the Rockox Triptych)
Peter Paul Rubens (1577–1640)
Koninklijk Museum of
Fine Arts, Antwerp

PAGE 55
**Christ healing the
Blind Man** (detail)
Francesco de Mura
(1696–1782)
Private Collection

PAGE 57
Portrait of a Young Man
(detail)
Sandro Botticelli
(about 1445–1510)
Palazzo Pitti, Florence

PAGES 58-59
**The Woman taken
in Adultery** (detail)
Guercino (1591–1666)
Dulwich Picture Gallery,
London

PAGES 60-61
The Redeemer (detail)
Raphael (1483–1520)
Pinacoteca Civica, Brescia

PAGE 63
The Magdalen Reading
(detail)
Rogier van der Weyden
(about 1399–1464)
National Gallery, London

PAGES 64-65
**Ars Moriendi: An Angel and
a Devil contending for the
Soul of a Rich Man** (detail)
Master of the Prodigal Son
(17th century)
Private Collection

PAGE 66
**Moonlight over the
Crimean Coast** (detail)
Ivan Konstantinovich
Aivazovsky (1817–1900)
Private Collection

PAGE 67
**The Prophet Nathan
admonishes King David**
(detail)
Palma Giovane (1554–1628)
Kunsthistorisches Museum,
Vienna

PAGES 68-69
**The Magdalen with
the Nightlight**
Georges de la Tour
(1593–1652)
Louvre, Paris

PAGES 70-71
The Crucifixion (detail)
Alessandro Castelli
(1809–1902)
Private Collection

INDEX OF FIRST LINES

PHOTOGRAPHIC ACKNOWLEDGEMENTS

For permission to reproduce the paintings on the following pages and for supplying photographs, the Publishers would like to thank:

AKG London: 24–25; AKG London/Orsi Battaglini 13; AKG London/Erich Lessing 20, 30, 32–33, 50–51, 67; AKG London/Rabatti-Domingie 10, 31, 34–35
Bridgeman Art Library: 22, 36–37, 40, 57, 58–59
Bridgeman Art Library/Giraudon: 4–5, 8–9
Bildarchiv Preussischer Kulturbesitz, Berlin: 18–19 (photo Lutz Braun), 38–39 (photo Jörg P. Anders)
The J. Paul Getty Museum, Los Angeles: 46–47 (94.PB.74)
© **National Gallery, London**: 16–17, 63
Scala, Florence: endpapers, 6, 28–29, 45, 54, 60–61, 68–69
Sotheby's Picture Library: 15, 23, 27, 42–43, 44, 48, 52, 55, 64–65, 66, 69–70